Robert McCrum

John McConnell
DESIGN

ACC ART BOOKS

Design series format by Brian Webb

Design: John McConnell © 2021 John McConnell
Text © Robert McCrum
World Copyright Reserved

ISBN: 9781788840873

British Library Cataloguing-in-Publication Data
A catalogue record for this book is available from the British Library

The author and publisher gratefully acknowledge the permission granted to
reproduce the copyright material in this book. Every effort has been made
to trace copyright holders and to obtain their permission for the use of
copyright material. The publisher apologises for any errors or omissions in
the text and would be grateful if notified of any corrections that should be
incorporated in future reprints or editions of this book.

The cover is a pattern made from playbill border patterns that
McConnell used on his Faber plays series.
Endpapers: Pattern made from his iconic 'ff' Faber logo.
Opposite: Self-portrait of John McConnell, 1985.

Printed in China
for ACC Art Books Ltd, Woodbridge, Suffolk, England
www.accartbooks.com

Design by Webb & Webb Design Limited, London

To Sam and Kate...

Self-portrait, 1985.

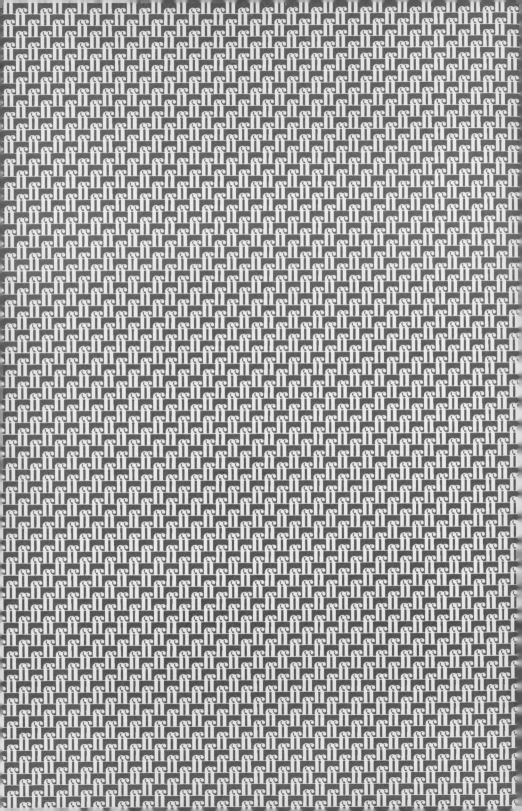

Introduction

I will probably never forget the moment in 1981 – a stuffy boardroom meeting – when John McConnell unveiled the future of Faber design. After two or three false starts elsewhere, and our list bursting with new young talent, from Kazuo Ishiguro to Marilynne Robinson, we were desperate for some contemporary artwork to mirror and promote the transformation we believed we were making. In the life of a great English publisher, this was a turning-point. The Faber board gave Pentagram the green light without much debate, but the decision was a bold one. For a blue-chip poetry publisher of Faber's grandeur to delegate its design to an internationally renowned partnership was like a vintage Bentley deciding to enter a grand prix. Rarely, in its distinguished 20th-century history, had the publisher committed itself to such a radical initiative. As Editor-in-chief, I had a ringside seat at this transformation.

Next to the ancient universities, the BBC, Fleet Street and the metropolitan clubs, Faber & Faber was a foundation stone in the edifice that housed a literary tradition. In post-war Britain, it was an influential part of the culture, badly in need of a face-lift. With the benefit of hindsight, the arrival of Pentagram at Queen Square was just part of a youthful creative insurrection, just as John McConnell was a leading member of a design revolution. After the bitter cultural crises of the 1970s, everything was about to change; and once the digital breakthrough began, there could be no going back.

In retrospect, we who became part of the Pentagram revolution at Faber were Thatcher's children, young, sleepless and slightly reckless. In 1983, when William Goldman published the Hollywood classic, *Adventures in the Screen Trade*, his mantra "nobody knows anything" seemed to capture perfectly the chaos, energy and irresponsibility of some exuberant times, the unintended consequence of a radical Conservative regime. This book will be devoured by students of graphic design, but it is also a portrait of a rare moment of creative innovation, a handbook to a great leap forward in which John McConnell and I were happy insurgents. What follows is his story and my part in it.

Robert McCrum

John McConnell is a designer who grew up with letterpress, thanks to his grandfather's gift of a printing press. These objects illustrate the lost world of his childhood. The metal frame is a 'chase' and the packing surrounding the

letters is the 'furniture'. Clamps were known as 'quoins' and the composing stick (above) was used for arranging lines of individual metal type.

Design
John McConnell

When John McConnell, the great British designer who's
synonymous with Pentagram, was very small, his deaf-as-a-post
grandfather, a printer's reader, introduced the boy to hot metal,
"three or four trays of type, and a thing called a composing stick".
However, the path to his vocation, and ultimately the design
revolution of the 1980s, was not quite so simple. And nor, when
you get to know him, is McConnell himself.

I worked alongside John at the publishers, Faber & Faber, during
the fabled Eighties. We were good colleagues and friends, who
enjoyed each other's company, but it's only now, in retirement,
that we have found the motive and opportunity to reflect on the
fascinating story of a career devoted to ink and paper.

In our digital and virtual world, John McConnell remains the
master of ink and folios, an artist of Caxton's craft. Possibly, this
can be traced to his origins in wartime London. He was born in
Balham, on the eve of World War Two, grew up in a flat next to
the tube on Bedford Hill, sees himself, and still sounds like, a
metropolitan, "an out-and-out Londoner", cultivating what you
might call a perky, demotic demeanour, like an artful dodger who's
about to sneak off to place an each-way bet on a good tip for the
2.15 at Kempton Park.

His mother Enid Dimberline had taught at Manchester Grammar
School. His father Don was a self-made accountant who loved
to read. John's childhood home was full of books, and a love of
literature. His appreciation of these riches, however, was severely
limited. "I fell in love with books," he remembers, but his ardour
was frustrated. Whenever he opened a book all he could do was
"look at the pictures." McConnell was – and still is – "extremely
dyslexic", an affliction he's spent a lifetime disguising. As a young

man, he admits, he was "silent and watchful", puzzling over such things as the silent "h" in his first name. The quest for identity is always the discovery of a personal story. As a dyslexic, deprived of the language with which to conduct this exploration, John turned to icons of design in the search for meaning.

In those far off days, to be severely dyslexic was to be classed as educationally backward, but John, a street-fighter who's as sharp as a tack, learned to camouflage his handicap, and find another narrative. It was thus, I believe, that he discovered the mundane politics of everyday life. There's no one I know who can better read a room: young/old McConnell possesses an uncanny grasp of almost any social or professional group-dynamic.

Like many lads of that era, growing up in wartime London, the boy John was fascinated by toy soldiers, but his instinctive take-away was singular. He would go to a toyshop, and make a beeline for the glass case with its row of tin soldiers. "I'd get out my sixpence," he recalls, "but they'd only give me one soldier." It was at this point that a tiny insurrection would break out in his youthful, and visual, imagination. "I didn't want just one soldier," he says, "I wanted the whole lot." Even at that early age, responding to the organisational signal of an army in uniform, he could see that visual authority derived inexorably from consistency and repetition, the thing we now call "branding".

"Visual signals," he instructs, "are what the army and the church are really good at."

Curious to find a higher loyalty than ink or type, I ask if he's a believer. "Is the church of any interest?"

"No," he replies. "I have no faith." His mother, to whom he was close, was "absolutely anti-Church." He recalls with pride that his sister, and all his brothers, were "never christened". Today, John keeps a house in France in the Petites Pyrénées. "I go to mass about once a year," he confesses, "because it's so incredible what the church produces, the creativity out of all that discipline." A resolutely secular man, McConnell has no appetite for the abstract torments of religious redemption.

In 1940, there was a more immediate kind of jeopardy. "I can still hear my father complaining about the Ack-Ack guns in Hyde Park, and see people with helmets, and I remember those Morrison [bomb] shelters. You'd have a shelter in the front room, built like a dining-room table, and you'd hide underneath it." These air-raid precautions became a kind of game. "It was a great excitement, as a child, to go to bed, hiding under a table," he recalls.

Perhaps this wartime play beneath the family furniture left its mark. As a boy, John proved to be outstanding at woodwork, a hobby he still practises in his workshop at home in Bayswater. It's what he does, he jokes, "instead of golf". Dogged by dyslexia, unable to compete in the 11 Plus exam that would have sent him to grammar school, he seemed destined for a more technical higher education. When the war ended, the family moved first to West Ruislip and then to Mereworth, a small village in the Weald of Kent. As a Londoner, with his brothers Dick and Tom, he felt "superior to the village kids, and I suspect we didn't give them much regard". Their parents ran the Mereworth store, the centre of village life, and John remembers his "first-ever commission", using his printing press to print a bag for the shop known as "McConnell's". Even as a boy, he had begun to think about the art of a singular identity. Meanwhile, battling with dyslexia, and labelled "sub-normal", John struggled into his teens.

One turning-point came at 12. His mother sent him for an IQ test, which he passed with flying colours. "Perhaps that did change me," he admits, "to find out I wasn't the dunce of the class." But he never ceased to feel like the odd man out: "I just wasn't the same as everyone else," he says. Next, young John was sent to Borough Green Secondary Modern. Looking back, he says he might have become "a tractor driver or something", but his woodwork teacher spotted some artistic potential, and urged his parents to enroll their son at art school in Maidstone, where John remembers arriving for his interview "in short trousers".

Art school at 14 was the making of John McConnell. A bright boy, with an exceptional IQ, he was finally leaving the humiliations of full-time education behind him, but still, he says, "feeling pretty bad about myself". Who can blame him? Throughout his childhood, he'd been written off as a dunce. But now he was in, and Maidstone College of Art would become his get-out-of-jail card, the passport to a new life: John loved art school (where the young Quentin Crisp was a life model).

"I tried everything," he reports. "Sideboards, long hair, short hair. I was terribly into a guy called Michael Cooper (who later worked with the Rolling Stones), an incredible photographer who was actually also in short trousers on the same bench outside the principal's office. I was impressed how quickly he adapted. Within weeks, it seemed, he was wearing a duffel coat, and sleeping rough under the local bridge." McConnell says he was a slow-starter, who still went home to his mum and dad.

Maidstone became a rite of passage, what McConnell calls "a classic art school, with a preliminary two-year course where you did a bit of everything: endless drawing, stone carving, life drawing, and sketch-book designing." After that, he had to decide where to specialise. He laughs mischievously. "In the end, I decided I'd become a graphic designer because the blokes on the graphic design course seemed more interesting than architects."

"Cooler?"

"Much cooler."

And there was another thing. The Sixties were coming, and someone had invented girls, apparently for the first time. "The girls in graphic design were all much prettier, and the guys in design wore those much smarter, Ivy League suits. Yes, it was cooler." Maidstone was also getting a reputation for typography. After Derek Birdsall joined the design department, from the London College of Printing, he would give John and his contemporaries a first-class grounding in type, plus some invaluable lessons in savoir-faire. "I still see Derek," he confides, chuckling again. "I mean, he taught me how to open a bottle of champagne."

McConnell left Maidstone College of Art in 1959, ready to enlist in Sixties London. "Up until then," he remembers, "it was the toffs who controlled the world, the guys with the posh voices, the

Norfolk jackets and the land. Then the pop industry burst
onto the scene, and suddenly our heroes were from Liverpool
and Manchester."

But first, he would enjoy one last flutter of teenage rebellion: six
months of draft-dodging. "I decided," says John with that hint of
steel I recognise from Faber days, "that I really didn't want to go
into the army for two years of National Service, so I ducked out
and went to Ireland. I had discovered," the artful dodger adds
gleefully, "that there was no extradition treaty with southern
Ireland [Éire].

Looking back, McConnell recalls "an amazing time" in Dublin,
with only the mildest anxiety that, on return, he might be arrested.
His father, back home, had been threatened by the police ("If your
son doesn't come back, sir, all hell will break loose, and your life
will be a misery."), and was advising young John to "come back
and face the music." In the event, there was nothing the authorities
could do, as the Mereworth village bobby (loose-lipped in the pub
one night) conceded. McConnell senior wrote to his son in Dublin,
"Stay in Ireland, and have fun." The Sixties were about to begin.

John meanwhile, returning to London, had met and fallen for
a glamorous Scots girl, Moira Macgregor, "an amazing draughts-
person from Dundee". They were married in Chelsea Town Hall on
1 March 1963, and celebrated a wedding breakfast of fish and chips
next door, at the Contented Sole. Soon after this, John set up his own
small business, McConnell Design, living over the shop with two
small children (Kate and Sam) in Paultons Square, Chelsea. John's
children have memories of their garden wall, an imposing brick
rampart that had once been part of Thomas More's estate. Moira,
to complete the picture, was becoming a highly successful fashion
illustrator working with Barbara Hulanicki, the founder of Biba.

While the Sixties exploded into multicoloured extravagance after
the drabness of the post-war decade, the young couple made their
way into a brave new world of *Ready, Steady, Go!* Their careers took
off, and John moved his office to Covent Garden. The famous
market was on its last legs, and was about to migrate south of
the river to Nine Elms. All around the semi-deserted piazza there

◄ ◄ ◄

The Biba logo, 1966. McConnell found inspiration for the design in a
Scandinavian type-book. His third model of the logo since Biba's beginnings in
1963, it has remained an iconic symbol of the brand for over half a century.

was cheap space for rent and – as always – the creative industry
(designers, publishers, typesetters, graphic artists and advertisers)
was moving in. The left-wing Thirties publisher Gollancz had
offices on Henrietta Street, the uber-literary independent Chatto &
Windus was in William IV Street and there, on the floor above the
new King Street premises of McConnell Design, were a couple of
book publishers, James Mitchell from Epping, and his partner John
Beazley, with some very big ideas about international co-editions.

McConnell has good memories of the young men he describes
as "the tenants upstairs". James and John (publishing as Mitchell

12

Barbara Hulanicki founded Biba in 1963. The brand challenged previous conventions of the fashion industry by selling youthful, trendsetting and locally made garments at unrivalled prices. Hulanicki experienced staggering success in the '60s and '70s, with stock in their Kensington Church Street store selling out twice daily at a time when most other retailers would do so twice a season.

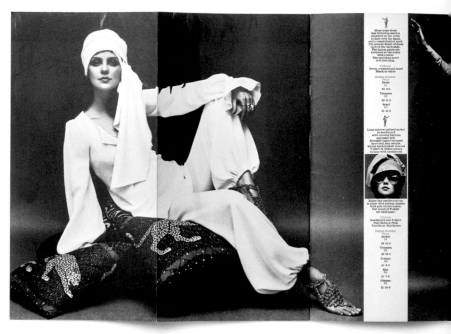

Beazley), he recalls, "understood the show-biz of books". When they went to the Frankfurt Book Fair, he says, "they didn't take a stand in the hall like everyone else, they took a room in a hotel near the fair, and invited publishers in with a glass of champagne. Then they would open a trunk to reveal the contents of whatever book they wanted to sell."

The title that Mitchell Beazley was selling in 1970 was *The World Atlas of Wine* by Hugh Johnson. Thanks to a commission from "the tenants upstairs", this became John McConnell's first big break. "In those days," he continues, "any book about wine was just pictures of cobwebs in some old wine cellar, with some bloke holding up a glass of vino. I was determined not to do that." *The World Atlas of Wine* was, for its time, thrillingly high-concept: notably low-key, and in some ways rather austere in its restraint, a plain burgundy background with a simple wine label displaying author and title in 20-point Latin Compressed. The whole point was, he says, that the cover "should look like a wine label".

McConnell defines his approach as "pragmatic", his code for understated and un-flashy. In his prime, he would often say that in a noisy, crowded and colourful market-place, the designer who had the nerve to lower the volume and restrain the display would attract the most attention. Now he says, "If you're in the arts business you're supposed to say, 'Ooh, darling, it's going to be lovely, and it'll be in *pink*.'" He always preferred to attract the attention of the market another way, saying, "Hold on, let's apply some thought here."

Hugh Johnson's bibulous compendium became an international bestseller with more than a dozen co-editions, putting Mitchell Beazley on the map. However, despite the huge success of *The World Atlas of Wine*, McConnell's streetwise cool was not to the publishers' taste when it came to their next project, *The Joy of Sex* by Alex Comfort. Laughingly, in a deliciously conspiratorial chuckle against the dullness of conventional publishing, McConnell recalls that "I saw this as a kind of AA manual on how to repair your sex life, while the book's editor was commissioning this hairy artwork and hiding it behind the filing cabinet in case the cleaners found it." He shrugs. "We finally fell out. Oh yes, I failed miserably." Was he bothered? It doesn't seem so. With lucrative commissions from Biba (thanks to Moira) and Penguin (thanks to his growing reputation for thoughtful book design) failure was not on the cards.

At first, McConnell came to Penguin to design the cover art for the fashionable (and dodgy) Seventies' financier Bernie Cornfeld's bestseller *Do You Sincerely Want to Be Rich?* (as told to Charles Raw). Something about John's cerebral approach to design caught the eye of David Pelham at Penguin who commissioned him to do a series of university monographs by contemporary European intellectuals such as Marcuse, Lacan and Althusser. It was here, he says, that "I really got my teeth into the idea of managing sixty book covers and developed the idea of designing a 'family' of titles."

The Penguin University series, with titles such as *Structural Anthropology* by Claude Lévi-Strauss, intended for college kids, was conceived as inexpensive but zeitgeisty. Streetwise McConnell cheerfully played to the no-frills concept by designing cover art with a matt black background – he's always loved black – a typewriter type-face (using his own Olivetti portable) and "found images" which required no fees. "I used to leaf through *Exchange & Mart*," he remembers, "and pinched tons of stuff from the *Whole Earth Catalog*. Then I'd wake up in the middle of the night and wonder if I'd get sued for copyright." Now his sly laugh has a hint of glee. "Touch wood, no one has ever come up and said, 'Oi, oi, guvnor. You've nicked my artwork.'"

John, something of a cheeky South London aristo, has always had a soft spot for classy outfits. It was Penguin more than Mitchell Beazley who gave him an appetite for book design. However, at this point in the early Seventies, his chief clients were Biba and British Aluminium. He was always fascinated by lettering. After one trip to the US, having spotted another typographical opportunity, he started Face Photosetting. Looking back on some transitional times, he recalls "a curious period between hot metal printing and the first computers". Contemporary innovations in type-faces were now being made on photographic paper. In a new market, appealing to advertisers, publishers and publicists, Face Photosetting became a cutting-edge business in which McConnell was both a partner and an executive director (working alongside Derek Robinson and Chris Dubber). Having been a one-man

McConnell has never been afraid to exploit a design cliché, and devise witty inversions of hoary old stereotypes. Bernie Cornfeld was a Seventies wide-boy, who was once briefly detained at Her Majesty's pleasure (for fraud), as well as being a Pentagram client. It's a fair bet that he never spotted how this design becomes an affectionate send-up of a questionable 'How to...' book.

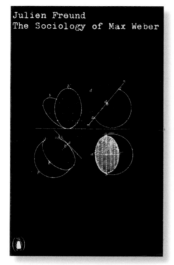

Julien Freund
The Sociology of Max Weber

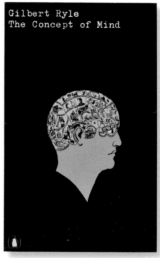

Gilbert Ryle
The Concept of Mind

Jan Vansina
Oral Tradition

Herbert Marcuse
Negations

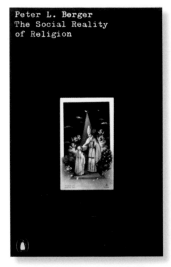

Peter L. Berger
The Social Reality
of Religion

Robert Langbaum
The Poetry of Experience

Barrington Moore Jr
Social Origins of
Dictatorship and Democracy

Claude Lévi-Strauss
Structural Anthropology

The Penguin University Series. This Penguin series, addressed to a
university market, and commissioned by David Pelham, marks McConnell's
first foray into a cover design that subordinated as many as 60 titles on
great contemporary thinkers, from Bertrand Russell to Jacques Lacan,

to a coherent design discipline based on McConnell's favourite colour (black) and his gift for improvisation (found objects). The series' typography had the elegance of simplicity: the setting of each title and author was derived from the keys of his Olivetti portable typewriter.

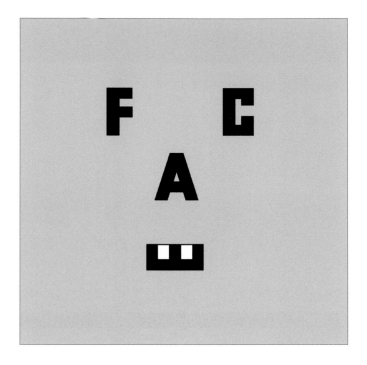

McConnell commissioned a number of designers, including John Gorham, to design an image for FACE.

band, it was now (for the first time) that he began to discover his interest in, and mastery of, "the politics of being in a business group." John's easy command of any office has been essential to his career as a pioneering designer.

Looking back over his long career, McConnell is inclined, sometimes, to see it as just one damn thing after another. "I was so bloody busy working, with my two assistants," he says, "that I never had time to surface." But then, in 1972, there was this memorable moment in King Street when he had a visit from "a guy named Alan Fletcher." This became another turning-point. Fletcher was a big man in all senses; roguish, celebrated and self-assertive. "He was a Libra not a Taurus, like me, but we certainly clicked," jokes McConnell. A no-bullshit design don, Fletcher was

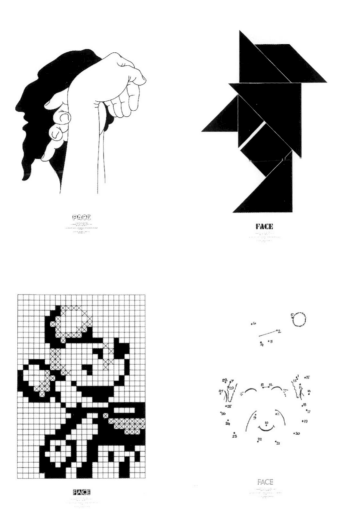

Face Photosetting was set up by Derek Robinson, Chris Dubber and John McConnell in London. FACE, the name derived from 'type-face', was a photosetting company which existed in the period between metal setting and the early days of computing.

These posters are rebuses of famous faces for FACE Photosetting. Isabella Beeton, Thomas Edison, Walter Raleigh, George Orwell.

Calendars for FACE.

also the co-author of *Graphic Design: Visual Comparisons* (1963), a trail-blazing volume he had written with Colin Forbes and Bob Gill, from whom John acquired his fascination with "cliché". At art school, his teachers had berated him with "That's a cliché, and you'd want the floor to open up," he says. "It was Bob Gill who taught me that a cliché is only an idea that's gone bankrupt through over-use. Bob would say, all you have to do is put more money into the account by reinvesting in the cliché, doing it a different way." His smile grows mischievous. "Clichés are very, very useful, you know."

Gill and Fletcher were young men like McConnell, designers who were putting graphic art to the service of thought. "They were my heroes," he says candidly. When Alan Fletcher turned up in the King Street office, he had a simple proposal. "Would I like to be his assistant?" To which John replied, "No, Alan, as flattering as that is, I wouldn't like to be your assistant." A beat. "But I would be a partner with you."

It was a bold counter-bid. Creative groups were very much in the air, and top dog Alan Fletcher had just founded the mega-cool Pentagram Design Limited in North Wharf Road, behind Paddington Station. Fletcher and his team were impressed. "Three or four days later," McConnell remembers, "his other partners showed up to check me out." Another ironical chuckle. Eventually, he was invited to become the sixth member of Pentagram Design Limited.

The year was 1974. David Bowie was singing "Rebel, Rebel"; the Tory government responsible for the "three-day week" was on the ropes; punk rock was in its infancy; the IMF hovering in the wings; and "Anarchy in the UK" just around the corner. It was perhaps not the most propitious moment to launch a design revolution.

Moreover, Fletcher and his partners nurtured the kind of elevated attitudes and aspirations that were – shall we say – a trifle alien to the graduate from Maidstone College of Art. "The first job that came to Pentagram when I joined was from Clarks shoes," McConnell recalls. His partners' initial reaction to this commission was to sneer at a "middle-class shoe company". McConnell's response was typically down-to-earth: "You silly buggers. I'll take it on." Which he did to great success, running Clarks shoes as a client through Pentagram and becoming a Clarks director. (In the end, he would also make John Lewis, Waitrose and Boots his clients.)

Experience is never wasted with McConnell. It was at Clarks that he got to grips, first hand, with all the issues he would have to address when he arrived at Faber. Now, it was John's office-political sixth sense that began to pay big dividends.

Any medium-sized company taking on an external "design consultant" would already be employing an in-house design department. McConnell learned that this in-house fifth column always presented the first big challenge. "The second you turn up," he says, "the in-house designers hate your guts because your appointment implies that they have failed miserably." Unfazed by this hurdle, McConnell would then set about figuring out his strategy. He often discovered that the in-house design department was the responsibility of "a dead-beat accountant" or – worse still – the marketing department, "because marketing is that pretty kind of stuff that has nothing to do with reality."

Once he had determined that he was dealing with a bunch of neglected designers who were being mismanaged by the wrong people in the company, he says he "learned very quickly to make friends with the in-house team," and to develop a cunning plan to transform their design methods. "If you don't," he adds with a laugh, "You're dead in the water."

It's worth noting, at this critical juncture in our story, that John's laugh is very much part of his design management character. It's not just a laugh, but a two-person conspiracy that somehow enlists you into an army of the elect: the thoughtful, savvy, design-conscious good guys battling Neanderthal forces of darkness. Applying a mixture of levity and deep thought to design, as usual with John, he quickly made friends and allies. He also promoted the idea of design within the company so that its identity and its "brand" became the responsibility of senior management.

◄ ◄ ◄

In the 21st century this is now S.O.P., standard operating procedure. In the 1970s, it was a radical innovation. When McConnell responded to overtures from Faber & Faber, he would embark on a design makeover that would test his resilience and ingenuity to the limit. To put it bluntly, the Faber & Faber that first made an approach to John McConnell, the Pentagram partner, in 1981, was up against it, a publishing legend in a hole. Worse still, two previous attempts at re-branding had left the management bruised and wary, with a lot of discarded artwork lingering reproachfully in dusty corners.

How best to convey the trouble the firm was in? Perhaps my battered, burnt-umber copy of *Waiting for Godot*, price five shillings (£0.25), tells you all you need to know about Fabers in the late Seventies. It offers the reader nothing so crass as a blurb, instead a long quotation from a *TLS* review ("Mr Samuel Beckett extracts from the idea of boredom the most genuine pathos and enchanting comedy") and because it's published by a literary imprint snootily removed from the hurly-burly of the market-place, this is not a paperback but a "Faber Paper Covered Edition". On the back of the book, there's an impressive list of other Faber playwrights: T.S. Eliot, Jean Genet, John Osborne and Tom Stoppard. An austere typographical cover projects an aura of avant-garde chic.

Even after a decade of intense social and cultural innovation, from gay liberation to punk rock, the literary eco-system to which this book belongs remains other-worldly, self-sufficient, eccentric and *sui generis*. Its ethos is at once distinctive and highly original. Beckett, the Irishman who wrote in French, the Nobel laureate who appears in *Wisden*, was a classic Faber writer: remote, reclusive and as rare as the hippogriff. His contemporaries on the Faber list included Philip Larkin, Ted Hughes, William Golding and Seamus Heaney.

If there were young Turks in the offing, they were newcomers like Christopher Hampton, David Hare and Paul Muldoon. Incredibly, almost the only woman writer on this august list was P.D. James (then in her late 50s). Deep in the Faber archive were serried volumes of 20th-century Anglo-American poetry and fiction (Auden, Pound, Joyce, Durrell) together with some weirdly commercial books on nursing and nautical knots, goat husbandry,

The 'ff' icon, now ubiquitous, was McConnell's masterstroke, a unifying logo that branded every new title with the publisher's identity. The italic version was used for Faber Music, a sister company. Again, its hallmark was simplicity, clarity and elegance.

the history of the potato, and folklore titles such as *Ask The Fellows Who Cut the Hay*.

At times, the Faber office in Queen Square seemed like a cross between a museum and a sanitarium. In-house memos would be addressed to "Mr Monteith", "Miss Goad", "Miss Mackle", or "Mr McCrum". There were many committees, jackets and ties. Inside this literary Vatican, until his death in 1965, T.S. Eliot had been the supreme pontiff. When I joined the firm in 1979, there were still some old hands with memories of "Mr Eliot". I can recall the formal side of a very formal organisation, as well as a lost world of manuscripts, Cow Gum, and carbon copies, galley proofs, telexes and Tippex, a poignant reminder of a book trade undergoing the biggest IT revolution since Johannes Gutenberg.

But change was in the air. A new generation had begun to break into the collegiate calm of the London literary scene. Julian Barnes, Peter Carey and William Boyd were being spoken of in the same breath as Martin Amis and Ian McEwan. The Groucho was replacing the Garrick. The first time I met Kazuo Ishiguro he carried a guitar and a portable Olympia typewriter, and confessed to feeling divided between short stories and rock music.

Here was Faber's problem: a generation of brilliant new writers was making its way to an imprint hopelessly trapped in the past, and wholly out of touch with the market-place. There was, however, a new MD named Matthew Evans who was determined to set the old firm, like a creaky man-o'-war, on a new course through the Roaring Eighties. His fellow director, the saintly John Bodley, was friends with Theo Crosby at Pentagram and, after a very few preliminaries, McConnell came on board with a commission to bring the house of T.S. Eliot into the late 20th century.

McConnell now says that, coming in to Faber in 1981, he was acutely conscious of the profound difference between words and images, two quite different media of communication. However, as usual, he cottoned on fast. In quite a short space of time, he had come up with the "three kinds of literary author" to whose cover-design wishes it became his responsibility to cater:

1. The Gravestone (severe typography dominated by the author's name);

2. "I Want a Matisse" (or a Picasso – the snooty desire for an item of world-class art to project a classic aura of grandeur and exclusivity);

3. "The Italian Bride" (based on the New York joke, "How do you spot an Italian bride?" She's wearing something old, something new, something borrowed, something blue, and something pink, yellow, orange and green).

Although the omens were quite good (Faber, with the Eliot estate, had just signed a contract for the Lloyd Webber musical *Cats*), McConnell faced some formidable obstacles. The Faber in-house design department posed a challenge McConnell had met – in microcosm – many times before. Faber's graphic designers were a law unto themselves, fiercely resistant to any kind of innovation. They had been trained by, and had worked under, the renowned Berthold Wolpe, whose typographical genius was universally acknowledged. No Faber designer raised in this Olympian atmosphere was ever going to pay much attention or respect to some unshaven "design consultant" from Notting Hill Gate. Actually, if they'd had insights into some of John's ideas about "cliché" and "repetition", some of these Faber stalwarts might have had a nervous breakdown.

At first, "McConnell" (as he was universally known) had a baptism of fire. Initially, I remember, he was allowed to re-design the company's stationery, but not much else. This he did, with typical flair, by introducing the iconic "ff" logo. This distinctive new identity would reflect the company's distinguished graphic tradition, which included designs by Eric Gill, Edward Ardizzone and William Morris. The "ff" also expressed a parallel narrative – its potent literary character – while the lower-case monogram conveyed a certain modesty and approachability, and an instantly recognisable trademark.

"Re-designing the letterhead for a great publishing company," John recalls, "was beneath the in-house designers' dignity. So...," he adds craftily, "I sneaked in through the back door without appearing to disturb what they [the designers] were up to."

Once inside, however, John went through this geriatric department like a wonder drug. He quickly discovered that within world-renowned Faber design only one designer, the redoubtable Shirley Tucker, had actually had any formal training (at the Royal College of Art, under Jan Tschichold). With his instinctive political sense, John made the marvellous Shirley head of the department, "turning" her to become his in-house fixer.

John was determined to break with the custom – endemic at Faber, but typical of publishers all over London – of book covers "getting designed in the corridor". This was the process, an informal tradition, by which an editor with some new cover artwork would take it round the house canvassing approving opinions from sympathetic colleagues.

McConnell established an all-powerful weekly "design meeting" (a kind of star chamber) chaired by Matthew Evans, attended by J. McConnell (design consultant) and R. McCrum (editor-in-chief), at which individual editors would nervously come and present their books by reading out design briefs about their new titles to a committee that also included sales and marketing, and the new head of an invigorated design department, Shirley Tucker. John would preside over these meetings with ruthless geniality, discussing cover briefs in a mood of take-no-prisoners. Then he and his assistant would take these deliberations back to the Pentagram studio in Needham Road to commission the artwork, and lay out the new Faber design.

Overnight, it seemed, after a decade of mediocrity and the tyranny of type (courtesy Berthold Wolpe), Faber covers were becoming energised and re-imagined by great contemporary graphic designers such as Andrzej Klimowski, Irene von Treskow, Pierre Le-Tan, Russell Mills and the dynamic duo of Sue Huntley and Donna Muir. In parallel with these innovations, John designed a series of sub-series, within the overall Faber brand: fiction, poetry, plays, film, music, etc.

◣ ◣ ◣

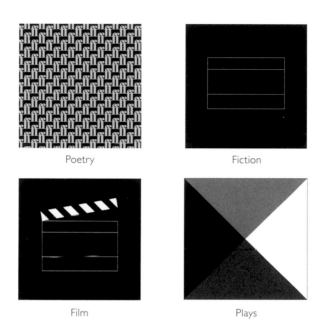

Poetry · Fiction · Film · Plays

In the 1980s, Faber's core titles – the publisher's unique selling point –
became a combination of contemporary poetry, fiction, film and play scripts.
McConnell created a template for each genre, using four separate series'
identities based on traditional design motifs.

Never short of self-belief, Pentagram had advertised itself as "multi-disciplinary, multi-national and multi-faceted", motivated by "a concept-driven approach that spurns the decorative or trendy". (Well, they would, wouldn't they?) By chance – and this was Faber's luck – the list we were creating in the 1980s, an age of irrational exuberance, was the literary embodiment of that manifesto. It was cerebral, high-brow (literary fiction), exclusive, international (many translations) and highly diverse. Our list and its "new look" (Pentagram) began to feed off and nurture each other in a perfect symbiosis. Words and images may have seemed in conflict when McConnell first appeared. But quite quickly, peace had broken out, and the awards began to flood in.

The change in the air turned disruptive. There was war (in the Falklands), industrial unrest (during the miners' strike), and a bookselling revolution (Waterstones). In hindsight, it was a radical and repressive Tory government that seems inadvertently to have sponsored a literary boom, with new names (Vikram Seth, Jeannette Winterson and Hanif Kureishi), new imprints (Bloomsbury) and loads of new money (soaring advances). This was also an international phenomenon inspiring a surge in new translations (Mario Vargas Llosa, Josef Škvorecký, Danilo Kiš), and new American writers such as Lorrie Moore (*Self-Help*) and Marilynne Robinson (*Housekeeping*), all of whom were published by Faber during the 1980s, and all with covers commissioned by John McConnell at Pentagram.

When these books began to win literary prizes (Booker, Pulitzer, Whitbread, etc.) the global publicity for these titles simply reinforced the Faber "ff" brand, and became that rare and intoxicating phenomenon, a virtuous circle of socio-cultural integration. Moreover, the discipline of McConnell's vision, which some authors found frustrating and over-schematic, had this consequence: it suggested to the attentive Faber reader a coherent publishing vision unifying the creative endeavours of all our poets, novelists, playwrights and screen-writers.

This of course was an illusion. There was, in reality, only a ferment of new writing by some of the most gifted writers of the moment. Occasionally, indeed, some of these would rebel, and (after much

McConnell claims to have forgotten this, but the cover design for the Poet Laureate's prose masterpiece on Shakespeare (a book that flopped badly on publication) saw a prolonged tussle between author and designer about the appropriate representation of the mythical beast found in *Venus and Adonis*, Shakespeare's re-telling of Ovid. Hughes liked to have a hand in the design of his book covers, and offered many examples of classical boar. It was a contentious part of the Pentagram discipline that such authorial interventions should not be allowed too much licence. On this occasion the score-line was Poet Laureate 0, Pentagram 0. Andrew Davidson's cover retains the hallmarks of a bloody compromise between author and designer.

in-house agony) reject the disciplines of Shirley Tucker and her minions. One *locus classicus* of this revolt was the enthralling case of the Poet Laureate Ted Hughes and his great book about William Shakespeare.

The Poet Laureate's lifelong obsession with Shakespeare had finally blossomed in 1990, with a commission for a work entitled *Shakespeare and the Goddess of Complete Being*. When the contract was signed everyone at Faber was cock-a-hoop. A new and controversial book about William Shakespeare? By the Poet Laureate? What could possibly go wrong?

When the typescript arrived in 1991 it turned out to be a rough beast of many hundred folios, encrusted with footnotes and manuscript amendments in Hughes' spidery black hand. Two poetry editors (one of whom retired to Oxford in disarray), and several copy-editors (one of whom had a nervous breakdown), grappled with an astounding document which was, in its way, a masterpiece of English prose, by a virtuoso of the vernacular. Many passages in the text had an astonishing majesty and insight. But it was also, not to mince words, impenetrable. Moreover, its dominant motif – the tragic, doomed boar found in Shakespeare's *Venus and Adonis* – had special place in Hughes' enraptured imagination, a whiskery creature that had become the object of his affections. The Poet Laureate wanted his version of this animal on the cover of *Shakespeare and the Goddess of Complete Being*, and he was in no mood to consider alternative visions. McConnell, Shirley Tucker, and their design committee had other ideas.

If you inspect the files in the Faber archive you will find a sheaf of roughs, some in colour, some merely in pencil, in which, going back and forth, Hughes and Faber battled over the right kind of boar. Needless to say, Hughes won, and the cover that emerged from this exhausting debate was an unholy compromise. This was, perhaps, The One That Got Away, a rare occasion when McConnell's Pentagram discipline did not prevail. And Hughes' masterpiece? It was published in April 1992, with many fanfares. The reviews were atrocious, and it sold very few copies. A first edition is now a rare, and highly collectible item.

◣ ◆ ◢

Two logos for the Swiss publisher Payot and the French publisher Éditions de l'Olivier. The P logo simply combines a traditional printer's paragraph mark. The olive tree is a McConnell trademark: it needs no explanation.

By chance, then, as much as design, Faber with Pentagram (McCrum plus McConnell) were in the midst of this irrational exuberance, making hay while the sun shone. A gold-rush atmosphere was mirrored in headlines: news of book prizes, launch parties, and the novelty of literary festivals. The chaos, energy and irresponsibility of this exciting transformation of the book world is half forgotten now, but for some of us, Thatcher's children, who were there at the revolution, the book covers reproduced here will bring back many memories.

And then, suddenly, it was all over. In 1995, I had a stroke, and survived, but withdrew from the firm to spend the next 20 years as the literary editor of The *Observer*.

John's post-Faber career has had many satisfactions. He has designed book covers for Phaidon and the Swiss publisher Payot. He joined The British Museum as a consultant to Joanna Mackle (he loves to work with young designers), and he continued to do the Pentagram Papers (a series of beautifully designed documents devoted to curious, entertaining and provocative topics, from crop circles and Mao buttons to Aussie mailboxes) he'd started in 1975. McConnell is proud of this collection which is part of Pentagram's DNA. "It still goes on without me, and it ties into the collector thing; it's a series bought by collectors. People like collections."

Now, in 2020, the world of books that John and I inhabited in the last century seems as remote and exotic as Beau Brummell and the Regency. Looking back, it was just a rare moment. We were young, ambitious and impetuous, and John McConnell was our guide to a vigorous new market-place. If, at the time, we had known how lucky we were, and what it really meant, we might have wished for it to go on for ever. But we were young and foolish, and we thought we were immortal.

We took it for granted that we should be reading a new Pinter play, or editing a Kundera translation, arranging to meet Ted Hughes, or Seamus Heaney, and marvelling over new artwork from Klimowski and Pierre Le-Tan. Such graphic design moments were inspired, decorated and organised by McConnell's remarkable visual flair. Perhaps only now do I realise how lucky and privileged I've been, to have had a front-row seat at this moment in book-design history.

John's conversation is still running on branding. "I do like collections," he concludes, with that incorrigible laugh, "which goes back, I suppose, to my tin soldiers." And, I'm bound to add, his immortal literary icon, the double "F".

"The collection of
Pentagram Papers
is inspiring and
demonstrates the
continuing invention
of this remarkable and
unprecedented design
partnership."

Milton Glaser

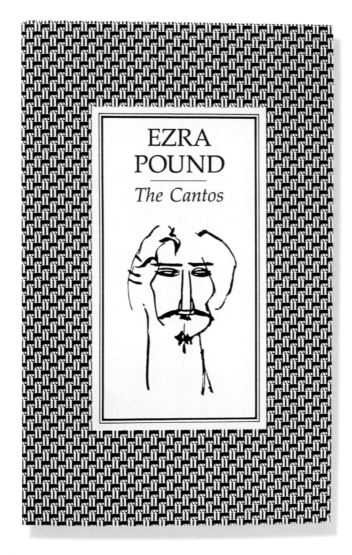

Faber poetry was always the publisher's crown jewels. McConnell's prize-winning design was based on what became known as the Faber 'wallpaper', a corporate setting for artwork appropriate to each poet's oeuvre.

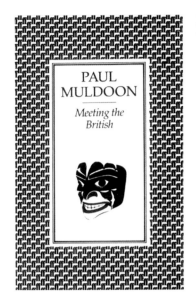

PAUL
MULDOON

*Meeting the
British*

SYLVIA
PLATH

Ariel

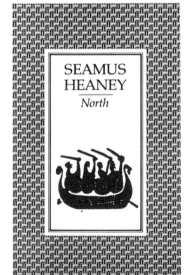

SEAMUS
HEANEY

North

PHILIP
LARKIN

*High
Windows*

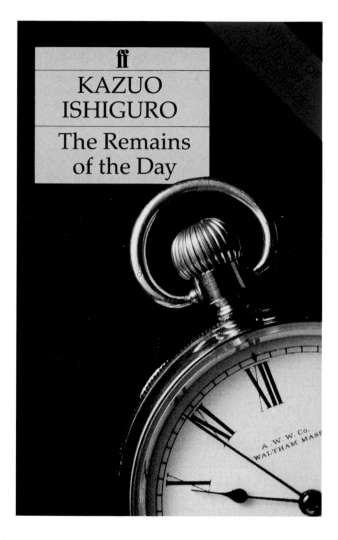

Cover art for contemporary fiction is as much a matter of mood as illustration: Pentagram was always highly intuitive about 'mood'. McConnell's approach to the young Ishiguro's prize-winning novels was to commission Sam McConnell to

photograph familiar images (an English pocket watch; a Japanese lantern) and subordinate this artwork to the discipline of the Faber fiction identity. When *The Remains of the Day* won the Booker Prize in 1989, the cover became iconic.

Andrzej Klimowski's covers for Kundera's fiction became a master-class in contemporary book-jacket design that was both commercial and classic. The author himself is a great admirer of Klimowski's artwork.

ff

MILAN KUNDERA

Life is Elsewhere

Irene von Treskow was another McConnell discovery. Her designs for these best-selling crime titles put P.D. James in a class of her own as a mass-market author with literary appeal.

ff

P. D. JAMES

The Children
of Men

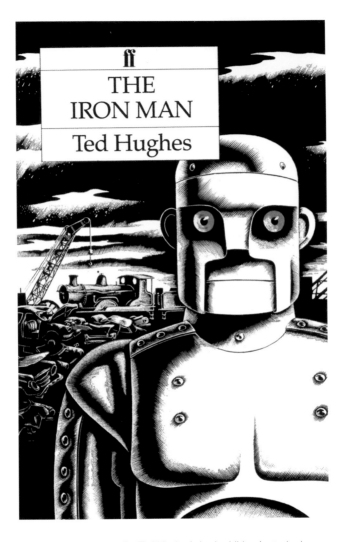

Andrew Davidson's covers for Ted Hughes' classic children's stories became another kind of mini-series within the Faber fiction list.

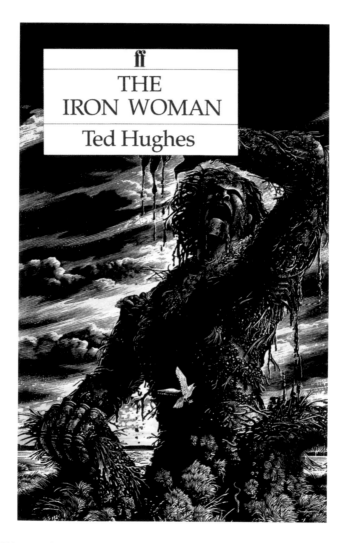

This cover for Ted Hughes' *The Iron Woman*, a companion volume, was also designed by Andrew Davidson.

ff

WILLIAM GOLDING

Lord of the Flies

Winner of the Nobel Prize for Literature

When William Golding won the Nobel prize in 1983, Faber had a heaven-sent opportunity to re-brand the novelist's impressive backlist, from *Lord of the Flies* to *Close Quarters*. McConnell commissioned new illustrations from the renowned artist Paul Hogarth in a deliberate pitch for a better class of reader.

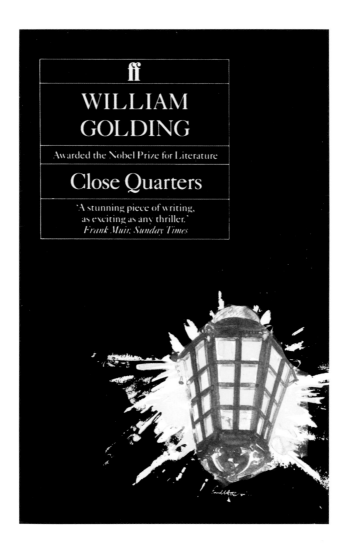

David Gentleman's covers for Lawrence Durrell's backlist became another example of an inspired marriage between jacket-artist and author. McConnell's use of the finest contemporary artists for Faber's classic titles subtly enhanced these books' presence in the market-place.

Paul Auster's UK debut in December 1987 put *The New York Trilogy* onto the bestseller list overnight. With Irene von Treskow's cover artwork, this volume of three novellas became a contemporary icon of 'cool'.

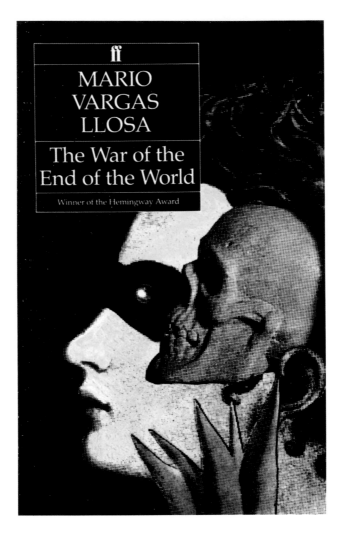

Andrzej Klimowski, as a cover artist, is infinitely versatile. Having made such a success of Milan Kundera's fiction, he managed to adapt his style to the magical realism of another contemporary master in translation, Mario Vargas Llosa, who

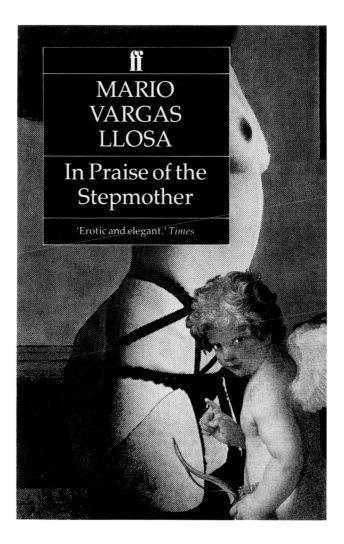

won the Nobel prize for literature in 2010. He is one of seven prize laureates (Golding, Pinter, Heaney, Pamuk, Ishiguro and Havel) whose work became associated with McConnell's book design revolution during 1981–1995.

Pierre Le-Tan designed artwork for the covers of two Garrison Keillor titles, *Happy to be Here* (1981), and his bestseller, *Lake Wobegone Days* (1985).

Michael Dibdin was a successful Faber crime novelist who wanted mass-market covers to increase his appeal to a mass readership. These elegant paperbacks – *Dead Lagoon* and *The Tryst* – designed by McConnell himself,

were his ingenious answer to author pressure for mass-market branding within a literary list such as Faber's.

These Pierre Le-Tan covers for Peter Carey's acclaimed fiction became
internationally renowned when Carey won the 1988 Booker Prize for
Oscar and Lucinda. Actually, the first draft of this cover presented the two
characters face-on in a way that Faber felt did not fully represent the charm

and magic of the novel. Everything fell into place once Le-Tan added the
playing cards. Subsequently, he designed artwork for much of Carey's later
fiction, and the two became friends.

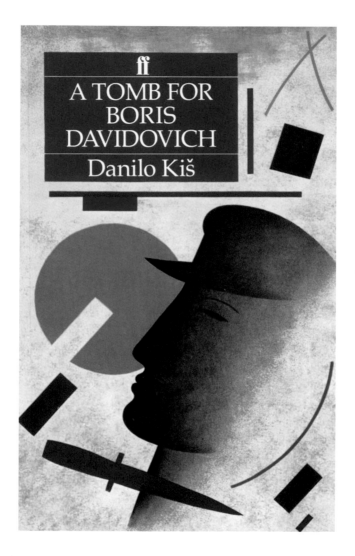

Danilo Kiš (1935–1989), a Yugoslav writer virtually unknown on
publication in the UK, is now recognised as a European modern master.
These covers by Paul Leith are a fine example of McConnell's skill at

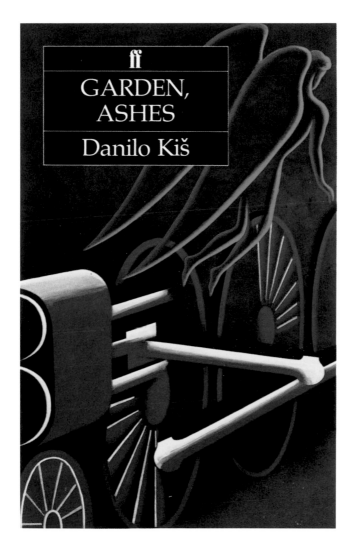

commissioning artwork that created a series-identity within the Faber list. Kiš could take his place alongside Kundera, Vargas Llosa and Ishiguro, but be distinctive, too.

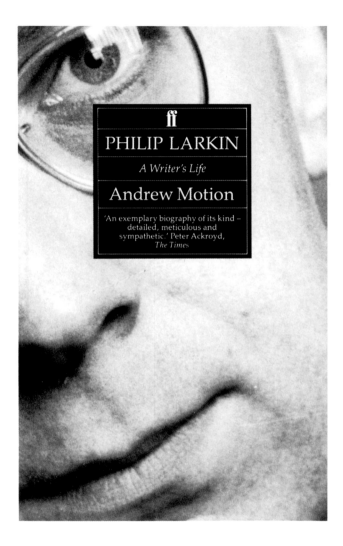

These Pentagram covers for biographies of Philip Larkin and Henry Kissinger illustrate McConnell's insistence on branding Faber books with the ever-present ff 'box'. He now says that, in his opinion, the 'discipline of the box'

enhanced the effectiveness of the image. This was not a universal view in
Faber at the time of publication.

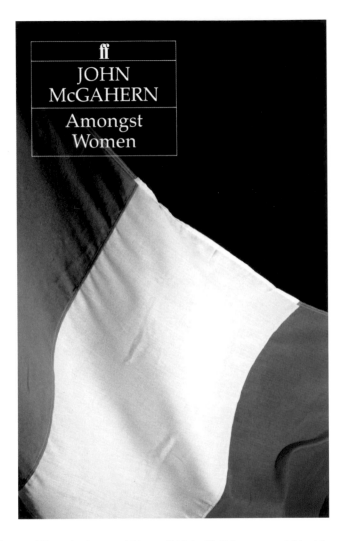

Amongst Women by the great Irish novelist John McGahern was published the year after the great success of Kazuo Ishiguro's *The Remains of the Day* (see p. 44). McConnell opted for another photograhic image and, ever frugal, commissioned his son Sam, as the photographer to shoot an Irish flag. Sadly the novel was only a Booker Prize runner-up, but the cover was widely copied by several foreign publishers.

Sue Huntley and Donna Muir designed this cover for Michael Tolkin's avant-garde thriller *Among the Dead*.

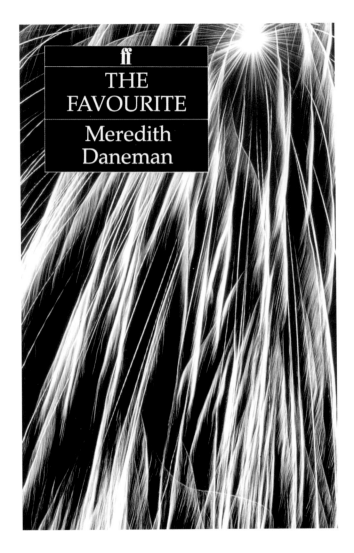

ff

THE FAVOURITE

Meredith Daneman

Meredith Daneman's elegant novel presented a challenge that eluded a succession of cover designers. Eventually, McConnell found a winning image for *The Favourite* in this photograph by Sam McConnell.

Mona Simpson is a renowned contemporary American novelist, the half-sister of the Apple guru Steve Jobs. This cover uses a 'found image' torn from a magazine, to establish the mood of the novel while not over-narrating its subject.

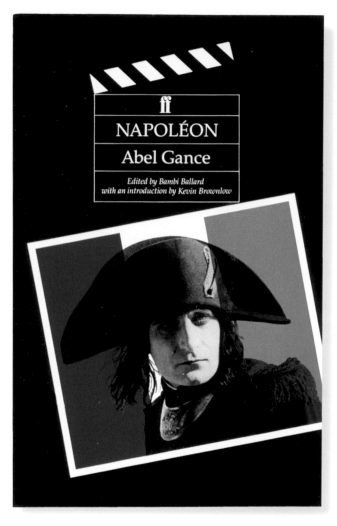

Covers for a series of Faber screenplays. McConnell utilises the visual cliché of the clapperboard by transforming the normal text panel. Images are placed at a jaunty angle to imitate the manner in which local cinemas would pin posters to their boards.

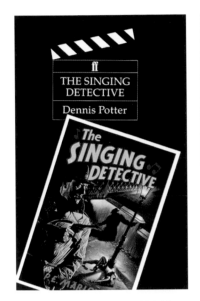

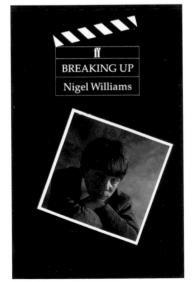

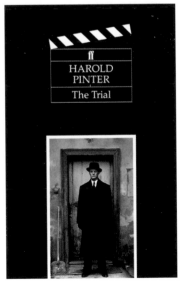

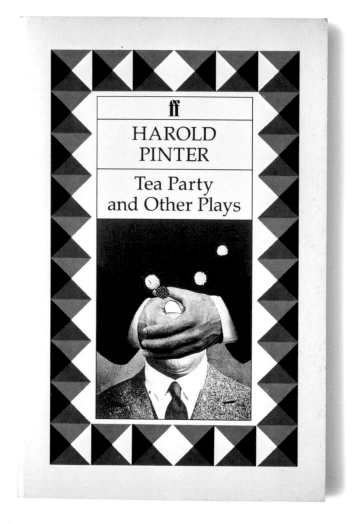

Covers for a series of Faber plays. During his FACE Photosetting years, McConnell discovered playbill border patterns in a catalogue of early woodblock printing. For this series he used the design as a pattern in the same format as the 'ff' pattern used for the Faber poetry series.

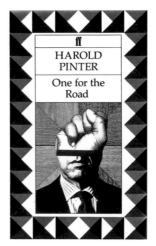

Covers for a series of Payot fiction books. Against a characteristically black background, McConnell commissioned portraits of the books' protagonists. They remained stylised in order to avoid interference with the reader's experience of the narrative.

Romans Payot

Robertson Davies
L'objet du scandale

Traduction de Arlette Francière

Covers for a series of Payot fiction books. The Payot mark designed by
McConnell represents a pilcrow or paragraph mark, which is the counter
inside the letter P.

Romans Payot

Michael Ondaatje
La peau d'un lion

Traduction de Marie-Odile Fortier-Masek

Le Châle Cynthia Ozick

Editions de l'Olivier

Les feux Raymond Carver

Editions de l'Olivier

Le dernier été russe Francine de Martinoir

Editions de l'Olivier

Une saison ardente Richard Ford

Editions de l'Olivier

**C'était
mieux avant
Howard
Buten**

**La
mal
élevée
Maya
Nahum**

**Falaises
Olivier
Adam**

**Les jouets
vivants
Jean-Yves
Cendrey**

Covers for Éditions de l'Olivier. The publisher's mark is conventionally on the spine of the book; McConnell has wrapped the mark around the spine. Together the series form an olive grove for your library.

PENTAGRAM PAPERS 27

Pentagram Papers will
publish examples of curious, entertaining,
stimulating, provocative
and occasionally controversial points
of view that have come to the
                    Pentagram.

PENTAGRAM PAPERS 21

CROP CIRCLES

Pentagram began Pentagram Papers in 1975, an exclusive series which celebrates brilliant ideas across the world, explored through curious and often obscure topics. Originally made to establish Pentagram as an authority and qualifier of intelligent design thinking, it was sent to colleagues, clients and potential clients. Pentagram Papers is continued to this day by Pentagram. Opposite: Pentagram partners group photo, Austria, 2004.

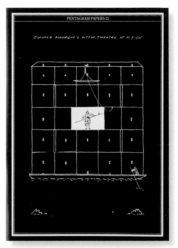

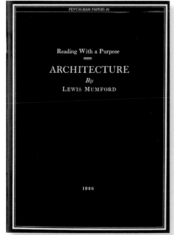

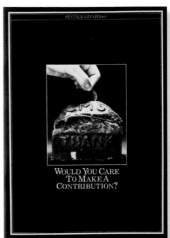

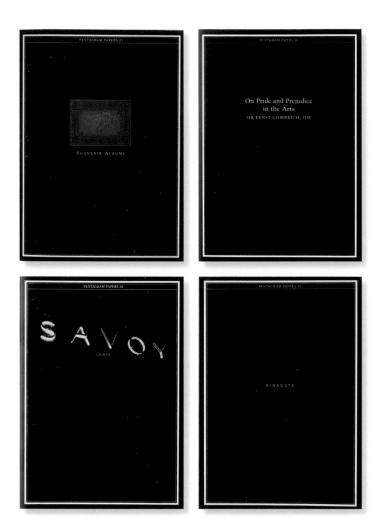

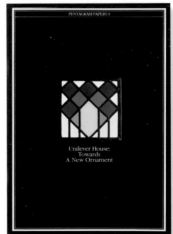

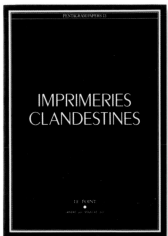

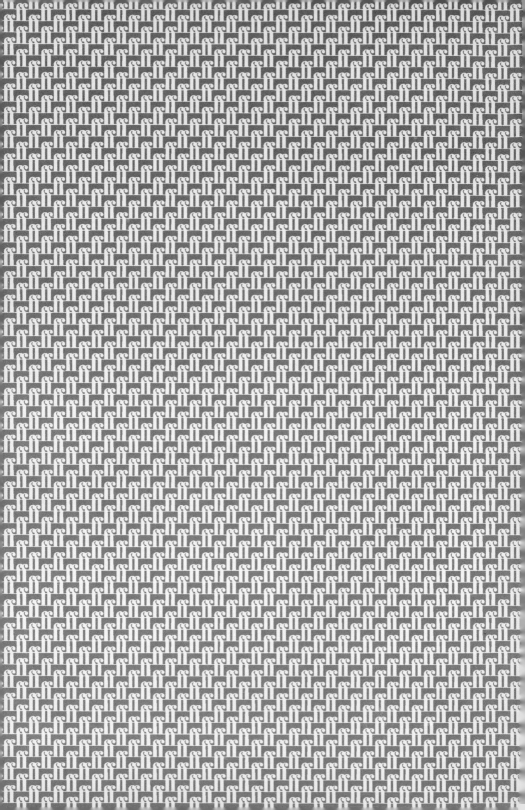

Acknowledgements

John would like to thank all his design
assistants who worked with him at Pentagram
and McConnell Design. Special thanks to
Alison Moore, his secretary for 26 years,
Flora Anderson, designer at Webb and Webb,
Margaret Pope for all her help, Helen Ingram
at Central St Martins, Tim Head, archivist at
Pentagram, Roger Stillman, photographer, and
Nick Turner, photographer, for their effort in
putting this book together.

For Robert McCrum's text, Gemma Robinson
was our indispensable research assistant.

Portrait of John McConnell, Zach John.